Stephen Anthony is Irish and married with two children. He lives and works in Toulouse, France. Prior to moving to France, he worked in England.

His hobbies include cycling, reading science publications, and writing short novels and poems. He would like to change the world with his work, influencing teenagers before they fall into the trap of the adult world where apathy prevails.

Stephen Anthony

BEAUTY IS TRUTH, TRUTH BEAUTY

AUSTIN MACAULEY PUBLISHERS™

LONDON • CAMBRIDGE • NEW YORK • SHARJAH

A CIP catalogue record for this title is available from the British Library.

ISBN 9781035825110 (Paperback)
ISBN 9781035825127 (ePub e-book)

www.austinmacauley.com

First Published 2024
Austin Macauley Publishers Ltd®
1 Canada Square
Canary Wharf
London
E14 5AA

To the cosmos; to its life supporting ability; to youth's purity and exuberance.

To my mother, a beautiful pilgrim soul; and my father, a beautiful mind.

To their love, which produced a stardust unique in the universe.

To my brothers and sisters: Stephanie, Damien, Caitriona and Anthony. What would I do without you?

To my upbringing that taught me the order of things. And the maxim: 'from each according to their ability, to each according to their needs.'

To my beautiful wife, Monia, my Habibi, who saved me from myself on many an occasion.

To our two sons, Hassan and Ahmed, our greatest creations.

To the importance of family.

To twenty-one Iveagh gardens and its occupants.

To all the people who helped me throughout my life
especially when my 'black dog' was raging.

To Doctor Albert Danan, who keeps the 'black dog' at bay.
To his secretary, Agnes.

To the French health system before the predatory politicians
got their hands on it.

Everyone with mental health issues deserves the care I have
had.

I would like to thank Austin Macauley Publishers for their help in getting this work published.

I would also like to thank all my family and friends for their invaluable support.

Names like Frank, Ronan, Mary, Grainne, Mark, Andrew, David, Richard, Peter, Paddy, and Olivier immediately come to mind that one found on life's journey.

Mammy, Daddy, Stephanie, Damien, myself, Caitriona, Anthony, Monia, Hassan, Ahmed, all the husbands and wives and children.

Venus of the Underground

A lonely impulse on my brain,
Svelte sylph enters train.
Gitanes on purple lips,
Versace on Stradavarian hips.

II
Raised arm, holding tightly.
Proserpine locks flowing lightly.
Rasputin eyes in dancing gaze,
At the passing billboard maze.

III
Bloused bosom, buttoned low,
Vulvous abdomen, bulging so.
Long, lingering limbs in parted posture,
A Rodin sculpture with rhythmic rapture.

IV
Gucci stilettoed cappuccino feet,
Take you to the vacated seat.
Harrods racing green on your lap,
People shouting, 'Mind the gap!'

V

Bronzed, unbending, beauteous bow,
You rise to go…No!
Svelte sylph exits train,
The only impulse on my brain.

London Underground –
An Irishman Reflects

As I read the lines Ich Och Irlande,
And Kavanagh's 'A Wet Evening in April',
I myself, was a hundred miles away,
In a land of morning tops and soft days.
Of rowan orange and furze yellow,
Fern green and golden meadow.
Red Geranium windowed whitewashed cottage,
Bog cotton on turf brown.
Such colour; Gauguin colour; Ballygauguin.
Peopled by old men in caps, who could read the weather
riddles,
And old women with ancient recipes in their head,
Of colcannon and griddle bread.
I left to make my fortune.
But all I see now is the fortune I left behind.

Ode to a Venus with a Sense of Humour

Throughout time,
The poets wrote of their muses',
Chestnut coloured hair,
Honey-dew eyes,
Coral cheeks,
Soft smile.
Svelte silhouette,
Gay gracefulness.
Earthy empathy,
Pilgrim Soul.
But never of their,
Sense of humour!
I know a Dulcinea, an Esmeralda,
A mellow mooded maiden,
Who makes us laugh,
With her zany humour.
To chuckle, to hum,
To *ronron,* what harmony!
Oh! Happy days!

So if reincarnation be,
Then all past poets
Will seek thee,
And re-write romantic poetry.

The Girl with the Waking Smile

This morning I woke,
To find a girl with a smile,
A waking smile,
Beside me.
Like some bodhisattva,
Straddled between,
Samsara and Nirvana,
To free my tethered soul.

Galway Girl

I see her now with dun hair,
Flung down her back like wetted otter.
A wisp, lone strand, wind swept across her,
Freckled dappled face.
And those soft sapphire eyes did glisten,
Like mist moistened cliff face.
Sweet scents from her womanly form,
Like rain drenched woodland of pine and fern.
Tinker, traveller, bohemian they say,
But all I see is a noble Peregrine.
Oh! Sweet Esmeralda that I long to know,
Alas! It will never be so.
I no Quasi Modo.
So long, forlorn, forgotten,
Fickle, freckled maiden.
Prufrock lives on.

Dancing Butterflies

Dancing butterflies,
Whirling and whorling,
Twirling and turning,
In a delightful display,
Of celestial play.
Like a binary star,
Seeking, searching,
Universal truth.
And I wondered,
If they wondered.
If their dance was,
A vertical enactment,
Of a horizontal desire.

Bannow Strand

On a Foxford rug,
In a rocky snug.
On a golden strand,
A woman, tanned.
Played 'Little Brown Jug',
On the village fiddle.
While a wide-eyed boy looked-on,
And laughed to see such fun,
Crying, 'Again! Again!'

II

A trawler's hand recounted,
A starless night spent,
On an anchorless boat,
On a stormy sea.
And taught us the meaning,
Of the word 'spooky'.

III

A woolly capped fisherman,
Brought his catch ashore.
And there I saw,
A shade never seen before,
A lobster blue. Heavenly hue!

Lemon Curd

In varsity jars,
She prepares,
Her wares.
Lemon curd as succulent,
As her soothing word.
While the blue serge suited man,
Delivers his daily pan.
And gives thanks to the Almighty,
For strong tea.
And strong women.
Amen.

Mind Seasons; Summer

Yippee, yappee, yahooee,
It's back!
The lights are back on in my head.
Not just that!
It's a fuckin' (veritable) firework display!
A shower of shootin' stars.
What more can I say.
Now stop think of those still before their darkest day.

Mind Seasons; Winter

When a manic depressive is depressed,
And he looks up at a clear sky,
On a still night,
He sees no stars!
And when he is manic and he looks up,
He sees no black.

Mozart's Clarinet Concerto: Adagio

Quirky, quarky, quavers, queuing,
Like waves waiting to break on shore.
Slowly, slowly, slowly soaring.
Wait, wait, wait.
Adagio, Adagio, Adagio.
Now! My little Nureyevs,
Jump, jump that synaptic gorge.
A million neurons resonating,
In perfect sympathy.
Like rustling reeds in riverrun.
Swooping, soaring, looping the loop.
Such tonal beauty, Iridescent.
Such colour! *Viola odorata.*
Effervescent, brain fizzle.
Shooting stars,
A supernova in my mind.
Oh! Mozart, puppeteer, pulled the strings,
Of sad thought through space-time.
From what unheard melodies did,
This moody meandering melancholy melody brew?

Keats, Van Gogh knew the rue.
Did the dove whisper in your ear?
Or did the deities take hold of your quill?

Minds in the Meadow

Head to head,
In a bed,
Of golden hay,
We lay.
Having a siesta.
Our entangled thoughts,
Tickling our,
Meandering minds.
Just to where,
Could two minds,
In love go?

The Woman on the Bog

Wild-eyed,
Raven-headed,
Pied beauty.
Scarlet Blouse,
Buttoned low,
Sleeves rolled up,
On Arms bronzed.
Stooped over,
A clamp of turf.
While her lover,
Sleans the bank.
Flicking soggy sods,
Out to be saved.
Some say,
She was a tinker girl.
But true beauty,
Knows no prejudice.
And love, less.
Under the midday sun,
They stopped,
To say the angelus.
After, for lunch,

They ate mustard dappled,
Ham sandwiches.
Washed down,
With milk from,
A glass bottle.
While watching,
Bog cotton fluffs.
Tremble in the breeze,
In this brown, blue,
White landscape.
Amidst a sacred silence.

The Rape of Gaia

I see you before me like Picasso's She-Goat,
Effete, emaciated, enslaved.
Suckled, silent, suffering.
Robbed of your oils and lustre,
My! How you have aged.
Pock marked coat, weal criss-crossed skin,
Open wounds on which us malignant maggots feast.
Crawling with lecherous leeches which you cannot shake,
With gentle tremors of your hide.
Consume, consume, consume. Uumh!
Om to oblivion.
The once majestic blue whale,
Is now but beached, bloated, blubber,
Puffing and panting in the last pathetic
Throes of life. And the Death rattle.
A silent scream across the universe,
In search of compassion and an end,
To this traitorous torture.
Or just a dignified end?
No! It is over. We cannot save you.

You are going to die.
For there is another coming, an evil weevil.
A billion times greater than anything,
You have known before.

War

In an Elysian field.
On a Carthaginian hill,
My wholesome American boy,
Lies. Shot full of holes.
His eternal reward,
The best view in town.
Blue sky; turquoise sea.
A tomb with a view.
At its head,
A cross in marble stone,
As white as young bone.
At its foot,
A pink bougainvillier grows,
Just above his toes.
Twenty-two; twenty-five,
Twenty-three; twenty-nine,
Twenty-four; twenty-six,
And himself twenty-one.
The young blood,
That trickled through,
The golden sand,
Of Hannibal's land.

As I left,
Some poppies wept.
The earth's sadness
At man's madness.

Graveside Flowers

Graveside flowers,
On hallowed ground.
Speaking to the departed,
In the language of plants.
The melancholy of purple pansies;
The tears of snowdrops;
The reawakening of daffodils.

The Unbearableness of Being

A howling wind raged,
And ravaged sulcri and gyri,
Of all happy thought.
Leaving a world, not as it ought.
A bleak, black, desolate, dark wasteland.
A no man's land without the others.
In the distance,
The death caw,
Of a lone crow,
On a one tree hill.
Here where time passes,
Grain by grain,
Like damp sand in an hourglass.
Stuck in a moment.

The Human Condition

Between a gibbous moon,
And a rising sun,
On a sleeping earth,
In an unfolding universe,
A spirit laden.
With weightless thought,
Looks to the heavens,
And contemplates his existence;
'Insignificant! And yet out of insignificance,
Is born such suffering!
The unbearableness of being.
The nauseousness of not.'
Another Pascal's paradox?

Achill

A geranium on the table,
Your dress on the floor,
And you in our bed,
Soul soothing selkie.
Detached, drowsy, dryad.
Your waking smile,
And dishevelled hair.
Your slender arm slipped,
From under the sheets,
Rests against the chair.
Fresher of the night,
Warmth of my life.
Sleep. Sleep softly,
To the ocean's om.

(Inspired by J. Prevert's Alicante.)

Anna Livia Plurabelle

A day before me,
And the beauty,
Of the city,
To discover.
Its *bukeshops*,
libraries,
galleries,
Concert halls,
Monuments.
Beckett bridge,
waiting for,
so and so.
Brobdingnagian,
Barber poles.
The waft of hops,
filling the still air.
Concupiscent ducks,
Iridescent in plume,
Preening on.
St. Stephen's Green,
Sheen of pond.
Cinemas, copulas,

the colour of her eyes,
the soft look of the just,
dominate the horizon.
A paperback reader,
Browsing your *bukeshops,*
Full of lovely *bukes.*
And loved you,
Anna Livia Plurabelle,
With a love that left all,
In its wake.

Woman

The honey-bee flew,
From flower to flower,
Searching the nectar *ephemere*.
While the humid sanctuary,
Of your secret garden.
Lured my id.
But my ego parched,
For the universal teachings,
That dress the weals,
Of a man's soul.
That pregnant moment,
Between man and woman,
The awakening,
Before to sleep.

Girl on a Bike

Entangled pair,
Off to where?
The breeze in your hair,
Without a care.
Your silken, slender limbs,
Dancing on a climb,
Such poetry; sublime.
Lines and triangles.
Arcs and curves.
Hue and sculpted form,
Chrysalis born.
Such sensual symmetry,
Divine geometry,
Venusian and Euclidean.
Bespoked Goddess,
Unchained temptress.
A Vesta in Chater Lea,
How you doth enchant me.

The Empress of Oxytocin

Suckled from my mother's breast,
An elixir rare.
I drank and drank,
From life's well.
And finding nothing to compare,
I drove myself to despair.
The only empress is,
The empress of oxytocin.

The dealers,
Sell their wares.
She-wolf, she bears,
To protect her cares.
The only empress,
Is the empress of oxytocin.

Cutting cords and strings.
'You'll be a man, my son.'
Empty cliché, rings.
No Spartan, brings.
The only empress is,
The empress of oxytocin.

Where are you mo chuisle,
From the womb,
To the tomb.
I long to hear,
That throb.
The only empress is
The empress of oxytocin.

Words Composed Upon a Bridge, Planet Earth

Screen preening apes,
Aswim in their silicon world,
Of well-thumbed bytes.
Modern day Narcissuses,
Seeking to sate,
Their empty egos.
On regurgitated data,
And likes.
What a sad reflection.
Ant-like procession,
To the altar of information.
These digitally devout dance,
To the tune of Boole's dogma.

Mistress Moon
(Or the Prisoner's Escape)

Oh! Mistress moon,
Out soon!
Silverlight monsoon,
Seducing lune, heart swoon.
Slipping through the clouds,
In some celestial serenade,
O! heady shade.
To wax, to wane,
To drive a man insane.
The tides are a changing,
Moods deranging.
Dark side, bright side,
Woe betide!
And in my cell I lie,
My prison…the sky.
Oh! Mistress moon so belle,
Soul soothing mademoiselle.

The Bitten Nail

My nerves at me again.
Nails bitten,
Down to the quick.
The half-moons of a lunatic.
This insane act of self-harm,
Where suffering becomes pain.
Searching soothing in vain.

The Mourning Mother

The loquacious lawyer defends,
The devilish dealer,
With the scheming sneer.
He holds court,
And in a suave spiel,
Pompously proclaims.
'Everyone has the right
To a fair trial.'
But the mother of,
The fair-haired boy,
Lying in her pieta arms,
Pleads, 'His father,
My lover,
A freedom fighter,
Starved to death,
To bequeath,
A free nation,
To his son.
But the great ideal,
Has become,
The greasy deal.
Legal appeal,

Ousts,
Heroic zeal.
Red wax seal,
Thicker than,
Blood red congeal.'

Reality

Are you the stage?
On which it all plays out?
All things past, present and to come.
Thought right, wrong and,
Not even wrong.
What stuff are you made of?
Unfolding like Matryoshka dolls.
Seeking, seeking quiddity.
In this theatre of dreams.
What reason do you
Need to be?

Abstract Poem

What thought,

Can we not convey?

When loquacious language,

Loses its way,

And we have nothing left to say.

II

What *hear, see, taste, touch, smell,*

Could Joyce's quill,

Not unlock the spell?

In what can we not dream,

Yet a hazy inkling,

Of becoming persists?

III

What brought nought into being?

And in a stroke,

Of pure abstraction,

Time became space-time,

Unfurling gravitation.

And in that pregnant moment,

It came to pass that,

The cosmos ceded its secrets to consciousness.

Abstract Poem

Oh! To write a poem from the inside out.
Not from the outside in!
With words that have been bet,
Into me like some apoplectic parrot.
In a cerebral smithy of arcs and sparks.
Where thought and language part,
And the colours of the soul start.
Where truth and beauty are one.
Is silence and nothingness that place?

Thirteen Magpies

'One for sorrow, two for joy…'
Today, I saw several lone magpies,
At various places, and instances,
Of the day.
Thirteen in all!
And I with my triskaidekaphobia.
Childhood notions,
Become adult superstitions.
They say God doesn't play dice,
And lightning doesn't strike twice,
But a quantum of mischance,
Collapsing all around me,
Is not beyond the bounds of possibility.

Cedar Tree

Green, low earth clouds.
Floating, abound.
Against a blue and white background.
And I reclining in your dreamy boughs,
Turning over leaves,
Like some Huckleberry Finn,
Up here out of the noise.
What poise!
The calm, the breeze,
The devil may care.
The petrichor.
Who are these dryads,
Coming and going.
The sap rising.